In memory of my Father,
who would have been 80 in 2007,
like Joseph Ratzinger.

To my Mother with affection and gratitude.

Many thanks to Fr Georg Gänswein for the
kind words he wished to give to the readers
of this book.

Story by
JEANNE PEREGO

Illustrated by
DONATA DAL MOLIN CASAGRANDE

Benedict and Chico

The Life of Pope Benedict XVI as told by a cat

Introduction by
FR GEORG GÄNSWEIN

CTS Children's Books

Benedict and Chico - The Life of Pope Benedict XVI as told by a cat: Published 2008 by The Incorporated Catholic Truth Society, 40-46 Harleyford Road, London SE11 5AY. Tel: 020 7640 0042; Fax: 020 7640 0046; www.cts-online.org.uk. Copyright © 2008 The Incorporated Catholic Truth Society in this English-language edition. Translated from the Italian edition by Pierpaolo Finaldi.

ISBN: 978 1 86082 493 7   CTS Code CH 12

Translated from the original Italian Edition, **Joseph e Chico - Un gatto racconta la vita di Papa Benedetto XVI:** written by Jeanne Perego and illustrated by Donata Dal Molin Casagrande. ISBN 978-88-250-1882-0. Copyright © 2007 by P.P.F.M.C. MESSAGGERO DI SANT'ANTONIO – EDITRICE Basilica del Santo - Via Orto Botanico, 11 - 35123 PADOVA *www.edizionimessaggero.it*

Introduction

by FR GEORG GÄNSWEIN

(Personal Secretary to Benedict XVI)

Benedict and Chico *is the title of the book that you are about to read, a book full of illustrations which will tell the story of somebody who is unique in all the world, the Pope himself.*

Many things are written and said about the Pope every day, but here, my dear children you will find something altogether different: a story told by a cat of all things! And it's not every day that a cat who is friends with the Pope starts telling his story.

The stories that Chico has to tell are well known and very interesting, and he tells them from his point of view, he is a friend of the Pope but after all he is always a cat.

I have been helping Pope Benedict for many years now; my name is Fr Georg (George in English) just like the Holy Father's older brother. You can be sure that everything you read in this book written by Jeanne Perego, illustrated by Donata Dal Molin Casagrande and published by the Catholic Truth Society is true and interesting. So I thank these friends of ours who have put together the story and the illustrations to offer a nice, easy read.

As I read the story I was intrigued and really felt that I could and would have wanted to say so much more! I can nevertheless share with you that the Holy Father is indeed a special person, but above all because he is a true friend of Jesus, and this is what matters most. This is the secret of his life, it is only when you become a real friend of Jesus that you can open your heart to the people you meet and to all the people who live in our world. Pope Benedict never stops reminding us all that it is love that brings joy and peace to the world and only God, who is love, can fill our hearts and give meaning to our lives.

The Pope is full of trust in Jesus so he never gives up, even though he is faced with all the problems of the world, and he never tires of loving all the people he meets. He has a special care for you young people in particular and knows that if you put your minds to it you can be really generous. He prays for you every day, that you may grow up in health and holiness, that way you will be happy and will be able to build a better world in the future.

The Pope also has a special care for cats and for all animals since they are all creatures of God, and often, like Chico, they teach us lessons we would do well to listen to. For example as Chico finishes his tale, he realises that the Holy Father is no longer just his friend but the great friend and guide of all the Catholics in the world. Even Chico, who after all is just a cat, understands the Pope's true mission: to be the friend of all humanity, loving everyone in the same measure that Jesus did when he gave his life for us all on the cross. But this is not just the Pope's mission, it is the mission of every Christian, of all those who choose Jesus as their greatest friend. This mission is for grown ups and also for children like you, because love has no age and knows no limits. Because love is God.

Vatican City, 4th July 2007   Fr Georg Gänswein

Benedict and Chico

MIAAOOW! My name's Chico, what's yours?

I'm a tabby cat, one of the most common cats you can find. I'm sure you've seen plenty of tabby cats around, but none quite like me, with lovely ginger fur and a great personality! So I'm a bit vain, but then again all cats are, didn't you know?

I've come to tell you about my best friend, a marvellous man with whom I've spent many happy times. He is an extraordinary person and I think his story needs to be told to as many people as possible. I'll tell you about where he's from, about how hard he worked at school and about what he's doing at the moment. I hope he can become your friend too. I'm sad to say that he lives far away from me now, because that's what human life is like. Sometimes they have to do things that take them far away even from their favourite cats. It's unbelievable, isn't it…

I heard that my old friend has such important things to do now that it would be difficult for him to come and visit me like he used to, and I'm sad about that. As sad as if they told me that all the mice in the world had disappeared.

But even if he can't visit me anymore, I'm sure he still loves me a lot. They tell me he asks about me sometimes, but I miss his stroking me and the nice things he would whisper to me in Bavarian. By the way, Bavarian is the dialect the humans speak where my friend comes from. I speak 'Cat' like every other cat in the world, but with a German accent!

My friend's story begins on the 16th April 1927. It was a very cold night… we cats hate the cold, and as soon as I feel the slightest shiver I go and sit in the kitchen, the warmest room in the house and the room where I decided to live. Because everyone should know that we cats choose our owners and not the other way around as I've heard it said. At 4:13 in the morning, in the house with number 11 on the door in the main square in Marktl am Inn in Bavaria, the loud cry of a newborn baby was heard. Joseph Aloysius was born; he was the third child of Maria and Josef.

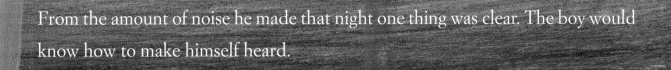

From the amount of noise he made that night one thing was clear. The boy would know how to make himself heard.

He was born on a very special day indeed, on Holy Saturday, the day before Easter. The next morning his mother Maria and his father Josef got ready to bring the baby to Church for baptism. Maria and Georg, his sister and brother ran around the house looking for their coats, but their mother told them firmly that it was freezing outside and she didn't want them to catch a cold. So the two little children stayed in the house pressing their noses to the frozen window pane until their parents, holding little Joseph tight, disappeared on the other side of the square.

My friend Joseph lived happily for two years in Marktl. Like all little children he would cry and cause trouble. Like the time when just before Christmas he saw a teddy bear he had set his heart on, disappear from a shop window in town. "Where's my bear gone? I want my bear!" he would scream, stamping his feet in front of the empty shop window. He was desperately disappointed, he'd been dreaming of that bear every night. He loved toy animals, he had a duck, a dog and a cat but that bear was the one he really wanted. He was soon in for a lovely surprise, when on the 24th December the children came down to join Josef and Maria their parents, to celebrate Christmas: who was sitting on the sofa, but the teddy bear little Joseph had been dreaming of.

Their peace and quiet didn't last long, and the family began a series of moves to new places. My friend Joseph's life would be full of changes and moves from one place to another. I don't know how he put up with it. We cats are creatures of habit and the very idea of moving to another place away from the smells and tastes of home is quite unacceptable. After all, have you ever seen a cat carrying a suitcase? All this moving around... it doesn't bear thinking about.

You see, Joseph's father was a policeman, his job was to make sure that everyone respected the law. He came home from work one day and told his wife: "I'm afraid we have to leave Marktl. I'm being sent to a town 30 miles away, but don't worry, we'll still have a nice big house where we can bring up the children." So all Joseph's family moved to Tittmoning.

My friend Joseph still loves that place, he often speaks of it. Once he told me of how every Christmas, he and his brother would build a lovely crib using moss and twigs and pebbles they had collected in the forest to make mountains and trees.

When he was three Joseph went to nursery school. One day while he sat in class, an amazing thing happened. In front of the school gate, a huge, shiny black car pulled up, (Joseph didn't know it at the time but that type of car is called a limousine). A tall man dressed in beautiful red silk all the way down to the ground stepped out of the car. On his finger he wore a big gold ring which flashed in the sunlight. The teachers told the children that this was the Cardinal who had come to confirm some of the children in the school. Joseph watched him carefully and suddenly shouted to his teachers: "When I grow up I'm going to be a Cardinal too!" He soon forgot about it though, and went back to thinking that when he grew up he would become a painter and decorator.

It was around this time that he started to go to the church near school, with his parents. He began to discover Advent and Easter and the other special times of the year that he would treasure for all of his life.

He was almost six when the family had to move again. At the beginning, Joseph, Georg and Maria didn't like Aschau am Inn, but as time passed they became fond of their lovely house with its big garden; it was the garden which Joseph liked best. There were many trees and beautiful coloured flowers and a pond where some fish splashed around. It was here that an awful thing almost happened. At that age, my friend Joseph never missed a chance of running around the garden at breakneck speed. Like all children he loved to run and jump, roll around on the grass and go exploring. One day as he chased his brother SPLASH! He fell into the pond. If they hadn't pulled him out in time he might have drowned. He learnt a lesson though, you always have to watch where you put your feet.

Joseph made his First Holy Communion in Aschau, where he also learned to play the piano. He liked the sound of the instrument from the first time he heard it, and playing the piano soon became his great passion. Even now that he's big, he still likes to relax by sitting in front of the keyboard and playing some beautiful pieces by his favourite composer, Mozart. I don't know much about Mozart but when I hear that music it makes me purr. When Joseph used to play I liked to walk up and down the keyboard for fun, and when he made me get down, I'd curl up next to him on the stool and purr away to the music, keeping time with my tail.

Believe it or not when Joseph was ten his family moved for a third time. They moved to Traunstein where his father, Josef had bought a house to retire to. When he first saw the house my friend was a bit shocked. It needed a lot of work doing to it. Joseph's mother needed to use all her skill to make the house look like a home. There was a big garden with a great many fruit trees, and a lot of space in which to play and have fun. The house didn't have many of the creature comforts which you humans now take for granted in your houses: there was no running water, so Joseph and the others had to go and wash at the pump in front of the house. Luckily we cats have an altogether easier way of getting washed, no need for soap and water. I don't think I'd have put up with all that coming and going just to stay clean.

My friend Joseph enjoyed studying more than anything else. He always had his head in a book and would read everything very carefully so that he didn't miss a single lesson that the book could teach him. That same year, full of enthusiasm, he started going to grammar school in Traunstein. It was a two mile walk to get there every day and the weather wasn't always very nice. I don't know how many times he had to walk through snow and rain to get to school.

It was here that he began to study Latin, an ancient language that we cats don't learn because we don't need it, but in Joseph's later life it would turn out to be very useful and people say he can speak it very well indeed. If you want to know what Latin sounds like I'll tell you: *mus* means mouse, *feles* means cat and *sinus* means bowl, like the one for my milk. These are obviously the three most important words in any language, so they are worth remembering.

In 1939 Joseph entered the seminary (a school for boys who might become priests) where his older brother Georg was already. It was a very important choice and the first step in a life dedicated to Jesus. It wasn't easy for the family to pay the school fees for two sons. Joseph's father was now a retired policeman with not much money to spare, but their sister Maria had found a job and was happy to contribute.

At first Joseph didn't much like life in the seminary with all the other boys training to be priests. He found it hard to concentrate with so many other boys around and there were lots of rules he had to keep. Then there were two hours of sport every day: jumping, stretching, running. It was a nightmare! I can quite understand, us cats don't like to do much exercise either, but you do need to keep in shape as you never know when you'll need to leap quickly onto a mouse, a cricket or even a dragonfly.

Just when Joseph and Georg were starting their life in the Church, something terrible happened in Germany which shook the whole world. A group of people called the Nazis came to power and began one of the most shameful and dramatic events in human history. Some of them did things that even the most ferocious animals would be ashamed of, and I know what I'm talking about, because when I have to, I can be pretty ferocious too.

At that time Joseph was forced to do something that went against everything he believed in, to join the army and leave for the war.

We cats don't have wars. If a new cat moves into the neighbourhood and shows an interest in a lady cat who's already taken, then we put on a menacing look, arch our backs, make our fur stand up, straighten our tails and hiss, and that normally solves the problem. Pity you humans haven't learnt to do that yet. Joseph was sent off to defend a factory that made aeroplane engines, and then to help build defences against a tank attack. He learnt all about fear in those days.

When the war finished Joseph was in a prison camp along with another 50,000 men. They had to sleep in the open and survive on a piece of bread and a ladle of soup per day. Luckily after only a few weeks he was free and began the 100 mile walk back home.

While he was walking together with a friend, a little van carrying pails of milk went past. It stopped and the driver asked: "Where are you boys going to?" "To Traunstein" they answered. "You are lucky I am going in that direction. Hop in the back. I'll take you." So Joseph and his friend were able to see their parents that very evening.

At the end of that year Joseph returned to his studies for the priesthood at the seminary in Freising. The building was in front of a beautiful Church which still has a special place in his heart today. He was happy with where he had ended up, especially because the big library had miraculously escaped any damage during the war and he could read and read to his heart's content. Although I've never liked worms very much, I would say that my friend was becoming a real bookworm.

As well as studying Latin, Joseph studied theology and philosophy, subjects that are a bit too difficult for us cats but which helped my friend get to know God better and about how human beings think. In no time at all it was time for him to go University in Munich. He was again plunged into an uncomfortable situation. The terrible bombings during the war had destroyed most of the building where he was supposed to study, so together with his friends, he was sent to a small castle outside the city which had been transformed into a temporary college. The lessons took place in the greenhouse where it was freezing cold in the winter and boiling hot in the summer. But Joseph was so happy to be there studying that he hardly noticed.

The castle was surrounded by a big park and when he wasn't busy studying, he would go for walks there. As he admired the trees and breathed in the bracing smell of the soil and wondered at the beauty of the sunlight streaming through the trees, his mind would return to what he was learning in his classes and to the important decisions that lay ahead of him; like his growing desire to become a priest and a teacher.

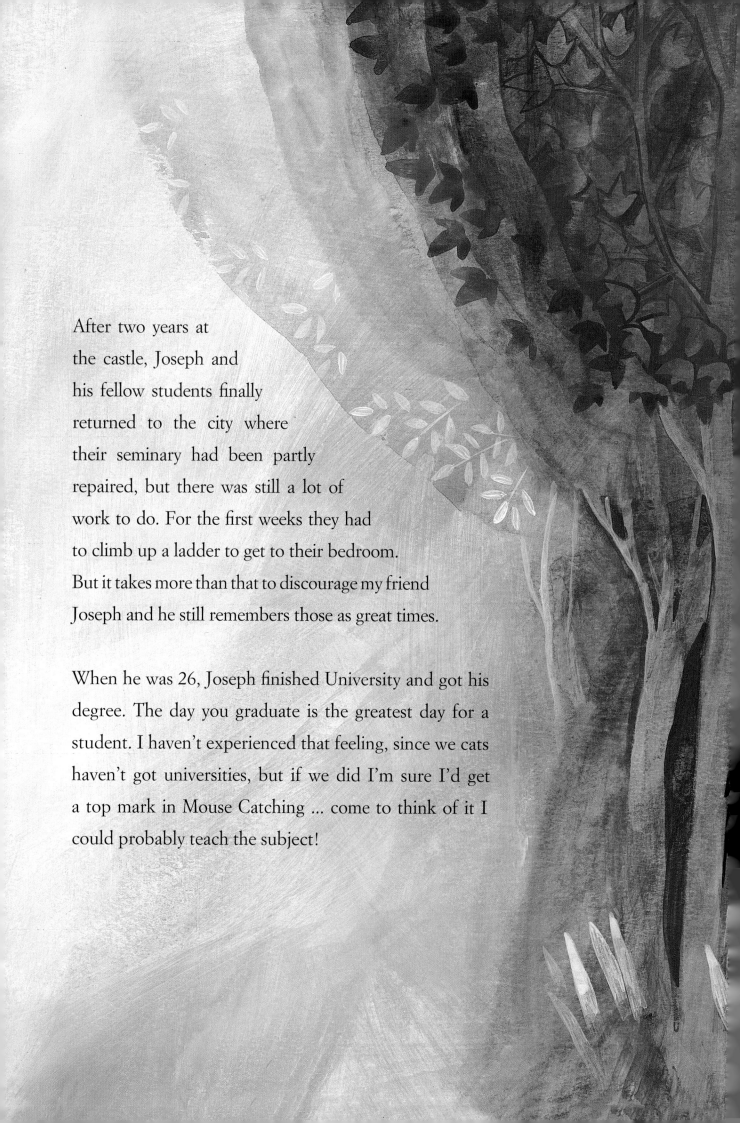

After two years at
the castle, Joseph and
his fellow students finally
returned to the city where
their seminary had been partly
repaired, but there was still a lot of
work to do. For the first weeks they had
to climb up a ladder to get to their bedroom.
But it takes more than that to discourage my friend
Joseph and he still remembers those as great times.

When he was 26, Joseph finished University and got his degree. The day you graduate is the greatest day for a student. I haven't experienced that feeling, since we cats haven't got universities, but if we did I'm sure I'd get a top mark in Mouse Catching ... come to think of it I could probably teach the subject!

In the meantime something of enormous importance happened to my friend Joseph: on the 29th June 1951 he was ordained a priest in the Cathedral in Freising, - the beautiful Church which was in front of the seminary. Joseph's brother Georg was made a priest on the same day too. The Cardinal laid his hands on the heads of those who were going to become priests, the very same cardinal that Joseph had admired so much that day when he was at school.

Whenever Joseph thinks of that day, one thing in particular comes back to him, and when he told me I was really moved by it. In the exact moment that the Cardinal lay his hands on Joseph a little bird flew up into the roof of the Cathedral singing merrily. Don't you think it was a special sign that my friend was going to be someone really important, and not just in my eyes?

Joseph started a whole new life, not as a student now, but as a teacher. He started by teaching in the same school where just a few years earlier he himself had been a student.

It wasn't an easy job to get and Joseph had to pass many tests to get it, but he wanted his parents, who were now very elderly, to come and live with him, and this gave him the strength to pass all the tests. So Joseph's house in Freising became home for the whole family including his brother Georg and his sister Maria.

It was in Freising that a bear appeared on the scene. What's a bear got to do with it you ask? Well it became an important animal for Joseph, almost as important as me, and he's had it with him ever since.

One thousand three hundred years ago, there was a Bishop in the town of Freising whose name was Corbinian. One day he packed his baggage onto a mule and set off for Rome on a pilgrimage. As he was travelling, Corbinian's mule was attacked and eaten by a great brown bear. Corbinian scolded the bear and told him that as punishment, he would have to carry his bags in place of the mule. The bear obeyed and followed him all the way to Rome carrying his bags, and on the way back Corbinian set him free.

Corbinian became a saint and the patron of Freising, and in memory of this amazing event, the bear with a pack on its back became the symbol of the city. Joseph never forgot this.

But let's get back to Joseph's story. Joseph was teaching and his family had moved in with him and we could say that they lived happily ever after... But no because there were other changes on the horizon.

My friend was a really great teacher, so good that he soon started teaching future teachers. He was called to teach in three different German universities.

In that time though, in all the Universities of Europe, trouble was brewing and protests were breaking out all over the place. Joseph didn't like all the trouble and wasn't happy with the whole thing. He was offered a job at the University in Regensburg where the students weren't causing any trouble. Georg had also just moved there as director of the choir in the cathedral.

So Joseph moved again and built the house in Pentling which is next door to where I live, and I got to know him there. Do you know how I understood that he loves cats? Because in his garden there was a statue of a cat, not a very handsome cat, but a cat nonetheless. If it had been a dog, I wouldn't have set foot in that garden!

During the day Joseph taught at the University and in the evening he would read or play the piano. His lessons were always packed, everyone wanted to hear what he had to say, he even became the deputy head of the whole university. One day while he was giving a lesson, a messenger arrived with a letter from Rome.

During the time he had been teaching, Joseph had written many books, and had often gone to Rome to help at meetings where all the Bishops of the world gathered together and decided important things for the future of the Catholic Church. There were so many things to talk about, that the meeting of Bishops lasted 4 years!

Having read his books and heard him speak, the Pope and his helpers realised that Joseph was a very clever man indeed. That's why the messenger from Rome had a letter with him which told my friend that he had been chosen to be Archbishop of Munich and Freising. Soon afterwards he also became a Cardinal, one of the Pope's special helpers.

Every bishop chooses a coat of arms to represent him. Joseph chose the crowned head that has been on every coat of arms of the Bishops of Freising for a thousand years; a shell which represents Saint Augustine, a saint that Joseph was particularly attached to; and a picture of an animal which held a special importance for him. A cat perhaps? Unfortunately not, although I think a tabby cat on a coat of arms would look wonderful. The third picture was that of the bear of St Corbinian, the one who carried a pack all the way to Rome. That animal really made an impression on my friend Joseph!

The story could have ended there, if Joseph had stayed in Munich until he retired to his little house in Pentling, the one with the statue of the ugly cat in the garden and the with the beautiful tabby next door. But there was a different future in store for him. The Pope was looking for someone to lead a very important office in the Vatican. Who do you think he called?

Joseph of course. In 1981 the Pope made him Prefect or head of that office. That's when he began to help and become a close friend of Pope John Paul II.

So Joseph moved again, this time to Rome. He was a little sad to leave his country behind, but happy to take on a new job. He worked harder than ever, writing books and articles, preparing documents, lessons and lectures. He organised meetings with important people, he studied, listened and spoke a lot and read even more. When he was really tired and needed a holiday he would come back here and rest in the house next door. I could always tell when he was back and would run to meet him and purr away. We had some great times together.

Sometimes I was a bit naughty and once at Christmas I even scratched him. He wanted me out of the house to get some fresh air, but I didn't want to leave my warm place on his sofa and so I scratched him. But he forgave me straight away: "Don't do it again!" he said, kindly but firmly.

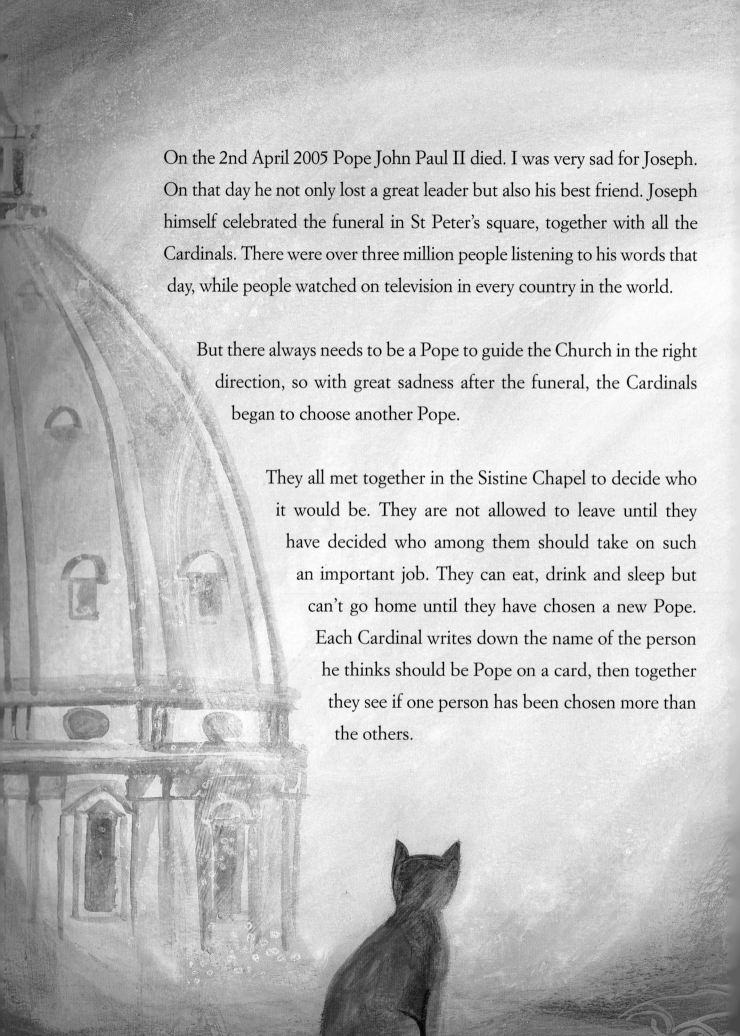

On the 2nd April 2005 Pope John Paul II died. I was very sad for Joseph. On that day he not only lost a great leader but also his best friend. Joseph himself celebrated the funeral in St Peter's square, together with all the Cardinals. There were over three million people listening to his words that day, while people watched on television in every country in the world.

But there always needs to be a Pope to guide the Church in the right direction, so with great sadness after the funeral, the Cardinals began to choose another Pope.

They all met together in the Sistine Chapel to decide who it would be. They are not allowed to leave until they have decided who among them should take on such an important job. They can eat, drink and sleep but can't go home until they have chosen a new Pope. Each Cardinal writes down the name of the person he thinks should be Pope on a card, then together they see if one person has been chosen more than the others.

If they have agreed on one person, the cards are burnt and white smoke comes out of a little chimney on the roof which can be seen from St Peter's square. If they haven't managed to choose then the cards are burnt together with a special powder to make black smoke come out of the chimney.

The white smoke which told the world that a new pope had been chosen appeared on the afternoon of the 19th April 2005. My owners, like everyone else were glued to their television sets. I thought they'd forget my supper altogether. So I sat with them and saw the white smoke on the television too.

A little later the window, where they announce the name of the new Pope, opened. Everyone was holding their breath... who could it be? Then the man responsible for making the announcement came out and said a long complicated sentence in Latin which means more or less: "Ladies and gentlemen, I'm happy to tell you that we have a new Pope. His name is Joseph Ratzinger and he's decided to call himself Benedict XVI". And a few moments later my friend Joseph appeared on the balcony.

In our house we were all over the moon, and in tears of happiness when we saw him greet all the people and thank the Cardinals for choosing him to succeed Pope John Paul II. I was so happy I forgot my supper altogether.

We've reached the end of the story and now you know why my friend Joseph doesn't have time to visit me anymore. Joseph isn't just my friend anymore: now he is the best friend and guide of all the Catholics in the world.

I'm just happy to have seen Joseph make the journey all the way from Marktl to Rome. He showed me how in life you have to work hard and never give up even in the face of difficulties.

Now I have to go. I have a feeling there's a mouse in my friend's garden, and you know what they are like... when the cat's away the mice love to play.

"Miaaoow! Say hello from me to the cats you know, and remember, be friendly to them, you never know if one of them might one day decide to tell everyone the story of another special person: you!"